Table of Contents

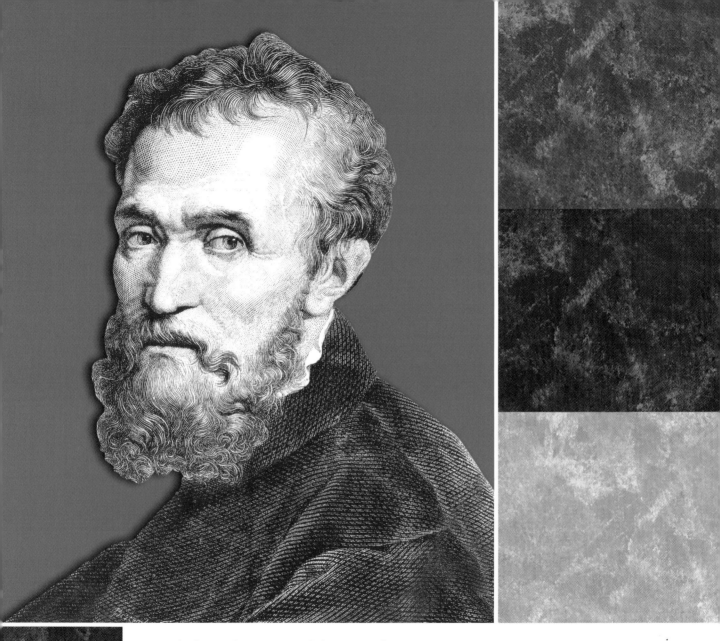

Michelangelo is one of the most famous **Renaissance** artists.
He was skilled in **sculpture**, painting and **architecture**.

Michelangelo and the Renaissance

Michelangelo Buonarroti (1475–1564) lived during the **Renaissance**. This period of European history lasted from the early 1300s to the late 1500s. During the Renaissance, Europeans rediscovered Greek and Roman **ruins**. They found old writings and art and studied them.

These discoveries helped change people's opinions. Before the Renaissance, art mostly showed people's religious beliefs. During the Renaissance, art became a means of personal expression. People began to show their ideas through their artwork. They also began to collect and value art.

The Renaissance began in Italy, where many Roman ruins are found. Raphael Sanzio, Sandro Botticelli and several other Renaissance artists came from Italy. Michelangelo lived in a region of Italy called the Republic of Florence. This area produced many famous artists, including Leonardo da Vinci and Giovanni Bellini.

Madonna of the Stairs is one of Michelangelo's early sculptures. It is a **bas-relief**, carved from a flat surface.

Young Michelangelo

Michelangelo was born on 6th March 1475, in Caprese, Italy. His father, Lodovico, was the mayor of Caprese at the time. Michelangelo had three brothers.

Michelangelo's mother, Francesca, was often ill and she could not look after him properly. Lodovico sent him to stay with a stonecutter who lived near Caprese. Francesca died when Michelangelo was six years old.

After this the stonecutter's wife took care of Michelangelo. He probably learned how to carve stone while living with the stonecutter. Later, **sculpture** would become his favourite type of art.

At the age of 10, Michelangelo moved to Florence with his family. His father sent him to school to learn how to be a gentleman. He wanted Michelangelo to become a great military leader or politician.

However, Michelangelo wanted to be an artist and at the age of 13, he became an artist's **apprentice**. He worked and studied with the painter Domenico Ghirlandaio.

Michelangelo studied sculpture in Lorenzo de Medici's school of art. Later in life, Michelangelo carved this statue for the tomb of Lorenzo de Medici.

Apprenticeship

Ghirlandaio taught Michelangelo **fresco** painting. Fresco artists painted directly onto a fresh, wet plaster surface. The paint soaked into the plaster and kept its colour.

Fresco painters began by creating drawings of their paintings, called cartoons. Apprentices traced the outline of the cartoons on the plaster with charcoal dust. They then sometimes painted sections of the fresco. These sections were usually on parts of a wall or ceiling that were difficult to see.

Ghirlandaio thought that Michelangelo was a talented artist. He sent Michelangelo to see Lorenzo de Medici, who ruled Florence at the time. Lorenzo enjoyed art and supported artists.

Lorenzo was impressed with Michelangelo's work and invited him to live at his palace and study with his sons. At the palace, Michelangelo met many famous artists, poets and scientists of the time. These people influenced him and his ideas about art.

In 1499, Michelangelo finished *Pietà*. It is considered to be his first masterpiece.

Pietà

Michelangelo studied human **anatomy**. He learned how body parts fit together. He even gained permission to study dead bodies at a hospital. He cut the bodies open to learn where muscles and veins were located. This knowledge helped him create life-like statues.

In 1492, Lorenzo de Medici died. Michelangelo decided to leave Florence shortly afterwards. People had heard about his skills as a sculptor. He was invited to work in Rome, where he was hired to carve a statue of Bacchus, the god of wine.

A church official saw Michelangelo's statue of Bacchus. He thought Michelangelo was a talented artist and hired him to carve a *Pietà*. This religious scene shows the Virgin Mary holding her dead son, Jesus Christ.

People were amazed at how life-like Michelangelo's *Pietà* looked. The folds in the Virgin Mary's dress looked very real and her face seemed full of genuine sadness.

Michelangelo wanted to show David thinking about his battle with Goliath. In this statue, David seems to look worried.

Return to Florence

Michelangelo's work in Rome had made him famous; now his work was in demand. In 1501, he decided to return to Florence, where city officials hired him to carve a statue. They had a tall block of marble for him to use.

Years before, a sculptor had begun to carve the Biblical giant Goliath from this piece of marble. Some of his chisel marks are still on the back of Michelangelo's completed statue.

Michelangelo decided to carve a statue of David instead of Goliath. David is the hero from the Old Testament, who killed Goliath with a slingshot. At the time, most artists had sculpted an image of him after he killed Goliath, but Michelangelo created a statue of him before the fight.

A shed was built around the block of marble so that Michelangelo could work on the statue during bad weather and at night. It took him nearly three years to complete *David*.

Michelangelo painted the Sistine
Chapel's ceiling (above). Ezekiel
(right) was one of the prophets he
painted around the outer edge
of the ceiling. People believed
prophets could predict the future.

The Sistine Chapel

In 1508, Pope Julius II ruled the Roman Catholic Church. He asked Michelangelo to paint a fresco on the ceiling of the Sistine Chapel in Rome. Michelangelo considered himself a sculptor, not a painter. However, during the Renaissance, the pope was a powerful religious and political leader. Michelangelo had to follow his request.

The Sistine Chapel's ceiling was nearly five storeys high and covered an area of more than 500 square metres. It took Michelangelo four years to complete. During this time he ate and slept very little, and his neck and back often hurt from looking up all the time.

In 1512, Michelangelo finished the Sistine Chapel's ceiling. The nine panels down the centre of the ceiling tell a biblical story. The first three panels show God creating the universe. The next three panels show Adam and Eve in the Garden of Eden. The last three panels show Noah and the flood. Michelangelo painted more than 300 human figures on the ceiling.

Michelangelo painted some of the people in *The Last Judgement* to look like people he knew. He even painted a wrinkled image of himself toward the centre of the painting.

Working for the Popes

Popes often asked Michelangelo to work for them. Pope Julius II asked the artist to make him a **tomb**. Michelangelo carved the statue *Moses* for this burial place. Pope Leo X was Lorenzo de Medici's son. He asked Michelangelo to design a church and a library for the Medici family.

In 1536, Pope Paul III asked Michelangelo to paint the Sistine Chapel's back wall, which covers more than 185 square metres. Michelangelo spent about six years painting *The Last Judgement*, which tells the story of the end of the world. Jesus Christ is shown surrounded by angels and saints. Below him, some people are rising towards heaven. Others are being pulled down to hell.

Michelangelo thought the human body was beautiful and he often created sculptures and paintings of nude people. Some church officials criticised *The Last Judgement* for including nudity. They hired an artist to paint clothing on the nude figures in the painting.

Michelangelo spent the last 17 years of his life working on Saint Peter's Basilica. He designed the dome that covers the church.

Saint Peter's Basilica

In 1527, King Charles V of Spain attacked Rome. This attack weakened the pope's power. The people of Florence then rebelled against the pope, because they wanted to rule themselves. City officials asked Michelangelo to design the city's walls and gates to protect Florence. During the Renaissance, artists were expected to study **architecture**.

As he grew older, Michelangelo sculpted less. He was not as strong as he was in his youth and carving stone became too hard for him. He spent most of his time painting, writing poetry and designing buildings.

In 1547, Pope Paul III asked Michelangelo to be the chief architect of Saint Peter's Basilica in Rome. This church is considered to be the most important Catholic church in the world. Michelangelo was 72 years old when he started work on Saint Peter's Basilica. He did not accept any money for this work because he believed it was his duty to God.

The Tomb of Pope Julius II is at the church of San Pietro in Vincoli (Saint Peter in Chains) in Rome, Italy. The statue in the centre is Michelangelo's *Moses*.

Michelangelo's Fame

Michelangelo died on 18th February, 1564, at the age of 89. He was buried at the church of Santa Croce in Florence.

Michelangelo is most famous for his work on the Sistine Chapel. In the 1980s, workers began to clean the chapel's ceiling. Many layers of dirt covered his painting and the cleaning took 10 years to finish.

Before the cleaning, people thought Michelangelo had used too many dark colours and that the painting looked gloomy. However, the cleaning showed that he had originally used bright pinks, greens and yellows.

Michelangelo is one of the world's most famous artists. His work influences many modern artists. They study his paintings and sculptures and sometimes learn techniques by copying Michelangelo's works.

Today, people travel to Italy from all around the world to see Michelangelo's art. Many of his famous sculptures are still there. *David* is at the city art gallery in Florence and *Pietà* is at Saint Peter's Basilica in Rome.

Timeline

1475 – Michelangelo is born on 6th March.

1481 – Michelangelo's mother dies.

1485 – Michelangelo's family moves to Florence.

1488 – Michelangelo joins Ghirlandaio's workshop as an apprentice.

1489 – Ghirlandaio introduces Michelangelo to Medici.

1492 – Medici dies.

1499 – Michelangelo finishes *Pietà*.

1501 – Michelangelo begins work on *David*.

1508 – Pope Julius II asks Michelangelo to paint the Sistine Chapel's ceiling.

1536 – Michelangelo begins to paint *The Last Judgement*.

1547 – Pope Paul III makes Michelangelo head architect of Saint Peter's Basilica.

1564 – Michelangelo dies in Rome on 18th February.

Useful Websites

www.michelangelo.com/buon/
This well-used website gives a detailed biography of Michelangelo. It also includes examples of his most famous works of art and explains how they tie into his life story.

www.talentedkids.com/art/art.php/
To find out more about Michelangelo and other famous artisits, visit the art pages of this fun, interactive website. As well as giving lots of information, there are many ideas for art activities.

www.kfki.hu/~arthp/html/m/michelan/
This top website displays a range Michelangelo's art; sculptures, paintings, frescoes, drawings and several of his architectural works.

www.christusrex.org/ww1/sistine/40-Judge.html
This unique website allows users to view magnified sections of the Michelangelo's famous painting *The Last Judgement.* Other pages on the site display more works of art found in the Sistine Chapel.

Note to parents and teachers
Every effort has been made by the Publishers to ensure that these websites are suitable for children; that they are of the highest educational value, and that they contain no inappropriate or offensive material. However, because of the nature of the Internet, it is impossible to guarantee that the contents of these sites will not be altered. We strongly advise that Internet access is supervised by a responsible adult.

Glossary

anatomy – the science of the structure of the human body
apprentice – someone who learns a trade or craft by working with a skilled person
architecture – the designing of buildings
bas-relief – a sculpture in which figures are carved or raised from a flat surface
fresco – a colour painting made on a wet plaster surface
Renaissance – a time of rebirth for art and learning, inspired by the discovery of ancient Roman and Greek ruins
ruins – the remains of something that has collapsed or been destroyed
sculpture – a three-dimensional work of art
tomb – a room or building that holds a dead body

Index